ALTAMIRA MUSEUM

EDICIONES
Aldeasa

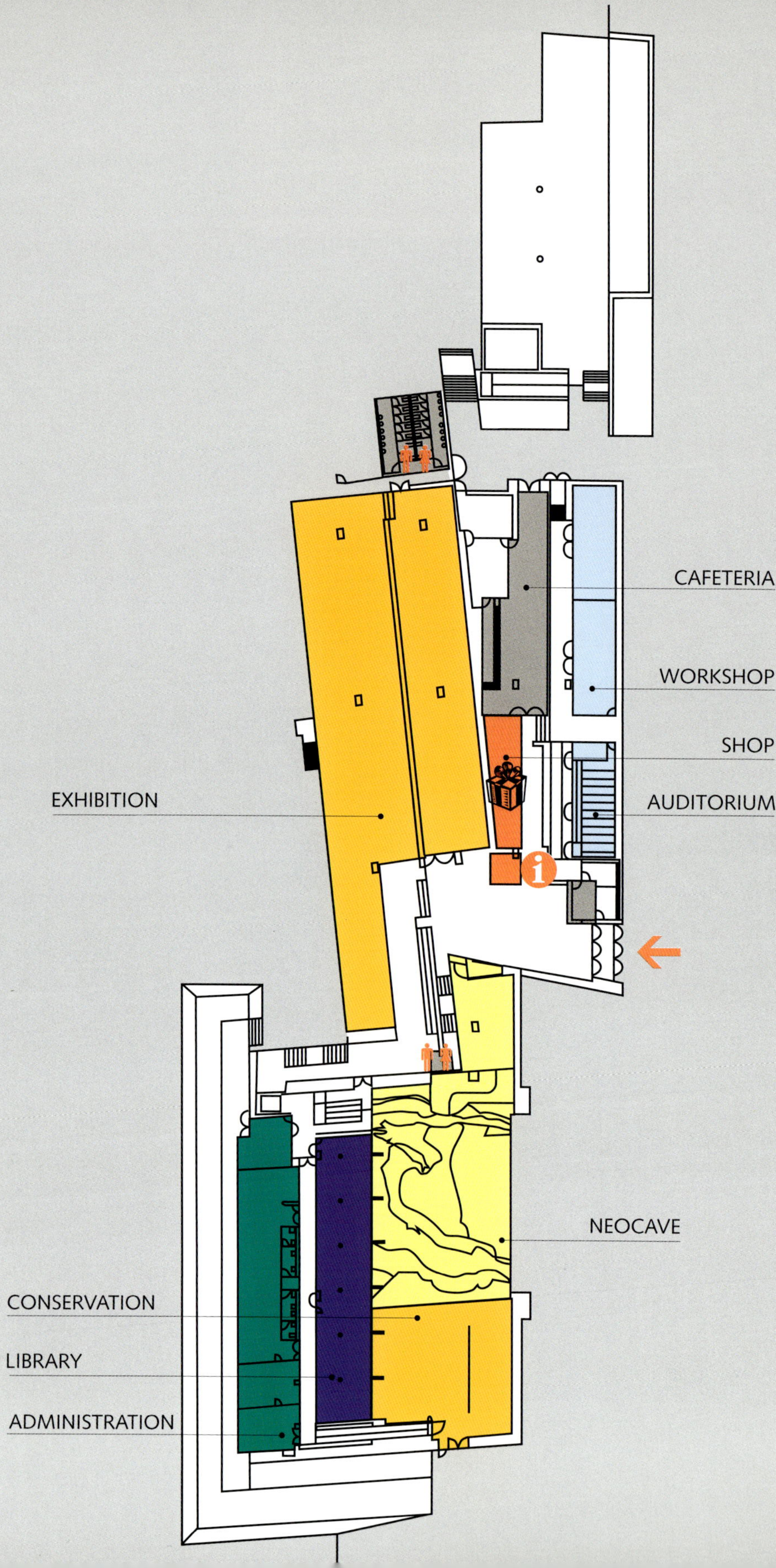
CAFETERIA
WORKSHOP
SHOP
AUDITORIUM
EXHIBITION
NEOCAVE
CONSERVATION
LIBRARY
ADMINISTRATION

ALTAMIRA MUSEUM

Floor Plan of Altamira Museum.

SUBTERRANEAN ART

Approximately 40,000 years ago, Cantabria began to be inhabited by members of the human species to which we belong, *Homo sapiens sapiens*. This species originally hailed from East Africa, from where its populations spread through Europe over a period of thousands of years. The arrival of *Homo sapiens* in Europe marked the beginning of the Upper Paleolithic, a cultural period characterised by the first manifestations of complex and abstract thought, one of which was art.

On the Cantabrian coast, our early ancestors found very favourable conditions for their way of life, which consisted basically in hunting and gathering food. The climate was cooler than it is today, though not as much as in central and northern Europe. The abundance and diversity of the flora and fauna guaranteed their food supply and the geological structure of the Cantabrian mountains, basically calcareous and therefore subject to karst development, was conducive to the formation of caves and shelters that provided refuge from the rigours of the climate. It is therefore not surprising that the populations of *H. sapiens* should have occupied a considerable part of the area during the Upper Paleolithic, as evidenced by the extraordinary number of caves showing signs of human habitation which have been discovered in Asturias, the Basque Country and, in particular, Cantabria, since the mid-19th century. The tools and implements found in these caves provide valuable information about the ways of life of Paleolithic man, and the notable collection of paintings and engravings on their walls and ceilings constitute mankind's earliest artistic manifestation. This art attained an astonishing degree of maturity during the Magdalenian period that preceded the major climatic change some 10,000 years ago marking the transition from the initial epoch of the Quaternary Period, the Pleistocene, to the Holocene or current epoch. The end of the Würm glacial stage brought milder temperatures, triggering substantial changes in the flora and fauna, to which man was forced to adapt. Over time, this adaptation translated into the so-called "Neolithic Revolution", which led to the emergence of agriculture and animal husbandry and, accordingly, to the ways of life and society that predominate today; initially, however, it merely sparked the disappearance of the societies of Paleolithic hunters and gatherers, and of their finely developed art.

A PLACE IN TIME

One of the many sites that was inhabited and decorated by man on the Cantabrian coast during the Upper Paleolithic was Altamira Cave, located in the municipality of Santillana del Mar (Cantabria). It lies on the upper part (156m above the current sea level) of the northern slope of mount Vispieres, which is made up of horizontal calcareous strata separated by layers of clay. Early karstic phenomena and the subsequent partial collapse of some strata gave rise to an underground area some 270m long comprising a winding succession of

Detail of the reproduction of the Polychrome Ceiling at the Neocave.

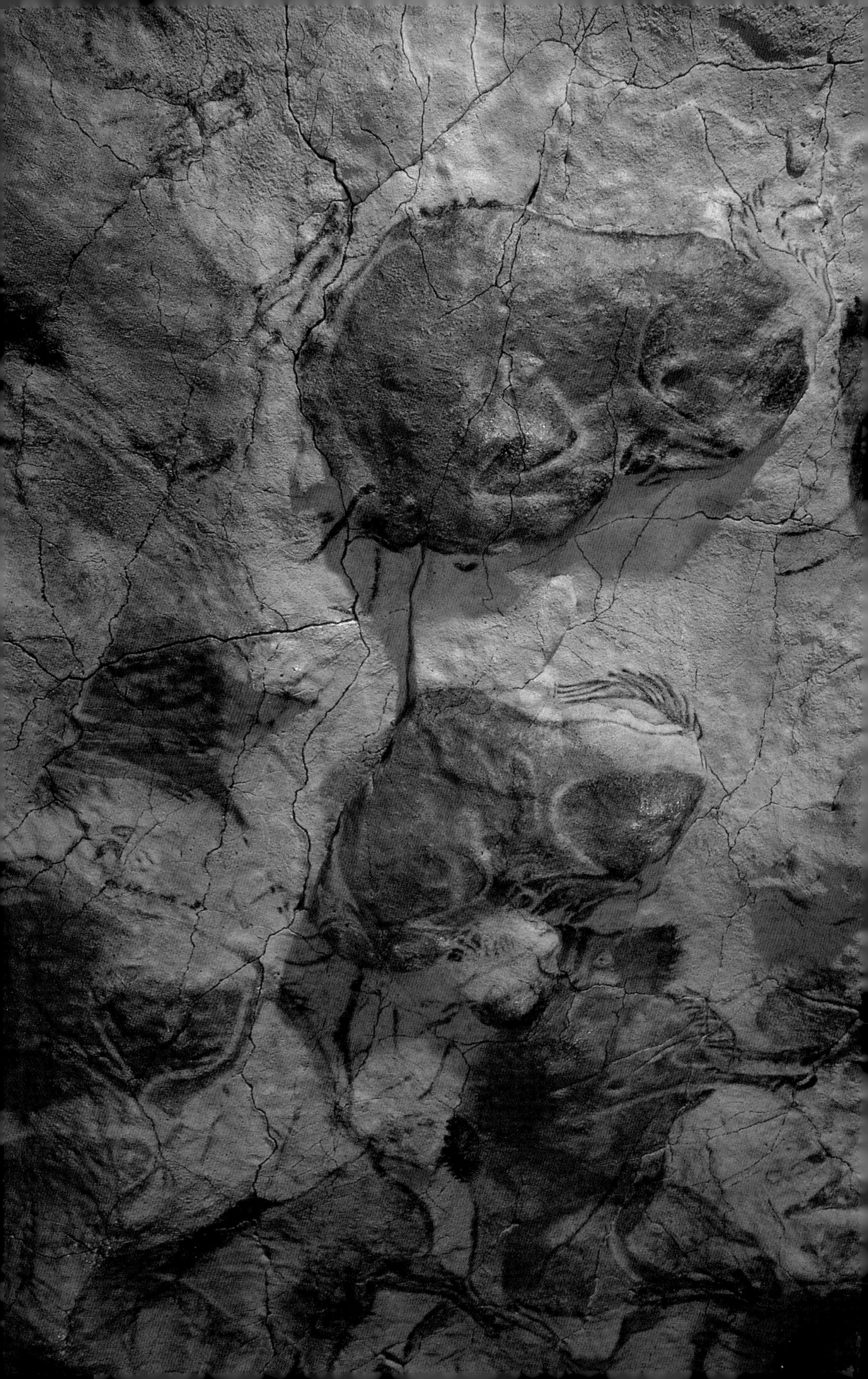

galleries and rooms whose height and width varied greatly. During the Paleolithic, the cave was accessed by means of a single rectangular opening some 15m wide and 2m high. Although its northward orientation did not afford its inhabitants the best protection from the rigours of the climate, this disadvantage was offset by its excellent location with respect to procuring food. At the foot of the cave lay the gentle valley where the medieval town of Santillana, probably a regular grazing pasture for the herds of large Pleistocene herbivores, now stands; the proximity of the valley of the river Saja, two kilometres away, and of the coast, at a distance of approximately ten kilometres (the rise in the sea level caused by the melting of ice following the Würm glacial stage has now halved this distance), enabled man to incorporate fish and mollusks into his diet.

The cave was occupied by man for two epochs, with a period of desertion in between: the first corresponds to the Upper Solutrean (18,500 years ago) and the second to the Lower Magdalenian (between 16,500 and 14,000 years ago). The human dwelling area was confined to the zone nearest the entrance, though abundant samples of cave art dating from both periods of occupation have been found throughout the rest of the cave, even in the Cola de Caballo (*Horsetail*), the innermost gallery that is hardest to reach owing to its narrowness. However, the examples of Magdalenian art are clearly superior, both in quantity and in quality. Shortly after the last occupation period, some 13,000 years ago, a landslide sealed off the cave's entrance, preventing it from being used and preserving the paintings intact for thousands of years. The modern rediscovery of the cave took place in 1868, and the superb set of Magdalenian paintings known as the Techo de los Polícromos (*Polychrome Ceiling*) was sighted in 1879. By some curious coincidence, the earliest example of Paleolithic cave art discovered in the modern age happened to be one of the absolute masterpieces of this art, and this was undoubtedly a key factor in the bitter controversy that arose in this connection and contributed to its tardy recognition by the international scientific community, which was reluctant to admit that "primitive" man should have been capable of attaining such artistic mastery.

PRESENT AND FUTURE

Since the authenticity of the Altamira paintings was universally accepted, their popularity has grown in proportion to their problems of conservation. When tourism became widespread in Spain during the 1960s, the cave came to be one of the most visited monuments in the country, together with the Prado Museum, and the first voices of alarm were raised warning that the excessive numbers of visitors were spoiling the paintings. In 1977 Altamira was closed to the public with the aim of undertaking an exhaustive study of the causes of the deterioration of the paintings and finding possible solutions. In accordance with the conclusions of this study, it was decided to restrict access to the cave, establishing an annual limit of 8,500 people, which has been maintained since it was reopened in 1982. To make up for this limitation, it was planned

General view of the Polychrome Chamber at the Neocave.

to create a highly faithful reproduction to disseminate knowledge of the cave's artistic richness to a much broader sector of the population. This decision was to lead to the Neocueva (*Neocave*), which was officially opened on 17 July 2001 together with the new installations of the Altamira Museum to which it belongs.

The chief concern governing the construction of the Neocave and Museum was to avoid endangering the original cave, located only 300 metres away, by ensuring its environment was not distorted by an excessive visual impact and, above all, by preventing any mechanical aggression which could alter the fragile balance of the limestone strata. For this purpose advanced technology was used, enabling the vibration levels to be maintained below what could be considered the natural level in the cave area. The building, designed by Cantabrian architect Juan Navarro Baldeweg, is laid out on horizontal planes which blend into the strata on which it is based, and this harmony is further accentuated by its pale stone facing, ochre plaster and even grass covered roofs. The interior, open plan and luminous, provides an impeccably sober backdrop to the permanent exhibition, which aims to show visitors the significance of Altamira as an archaeological site of primary importance and the keys to the Paleolithic world in which the men who inhabited and decorated it lived.

THE NEOCAVE

The Neocave was built to enable all those who visit Altamira to see the paintings in the context in which they were created. It is a replica of the most interesting parts of the original cave and recreates the textures, contours and colour variations down to the last millimetre and, in the case of the paintings, even employs the same natural pigments used by the primitive artists. Before going inside, we are shown a film which briefly examines the main milestones in the history of the cave, including the two periods of occupation by Paleolithic man and the in-between period when it was deserted, the landslide which sealed off its entrance, its subsequent rediscovery and the vicissitudes which led to its closure and reopening under restricted visiting conditions last century.

The first area we come to is the **Magdalenian settlement** located in the wide entrance vestibule by the cave's mouth. A virtual projection gives us an idea of how the hunters who inhabited Altamira 14,500 years ago lived. Further on, the **archaeological excavation** shows the methods of field research used to obtain the information we have on the cave dwellers. We thus see how the succession of strata indicates the phases of occupation: one during the Solutrean, which has been attributed an age of 18,500 years; and another during the Magdalenian, 14,500 years ago; and between them a period in which it was deserted, as evidenced by a layer of sterile clay.

Basically, three archaeological excavation campaigns have been conducted at Altamira: those led by Marcelino Sanz de Sautuola between 1876 and 1879, the year he discovered the paintings of the Polychrome Ceiling; those of Cantabrian

Bison (above) and large hind (below) from the Polychrome Ceiling, reproduced at the Neocave.

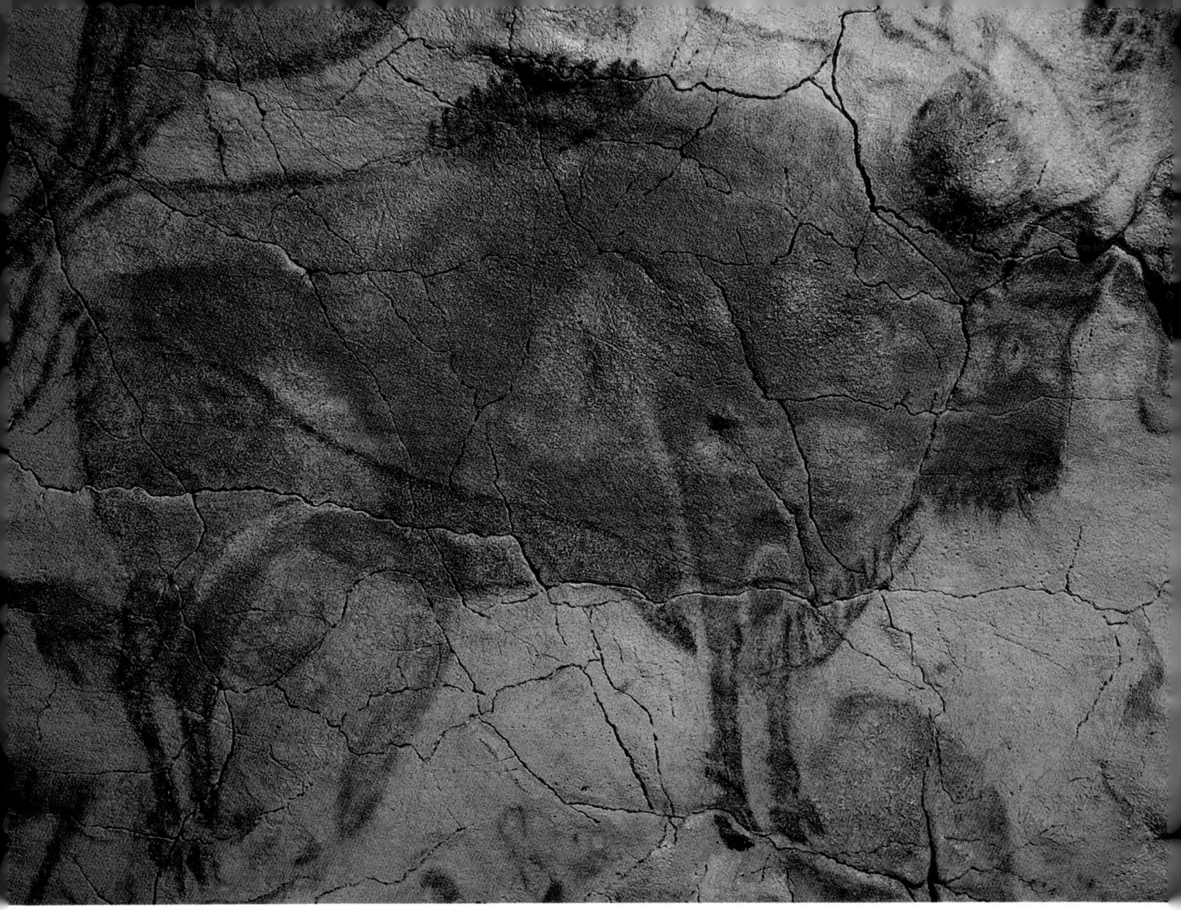

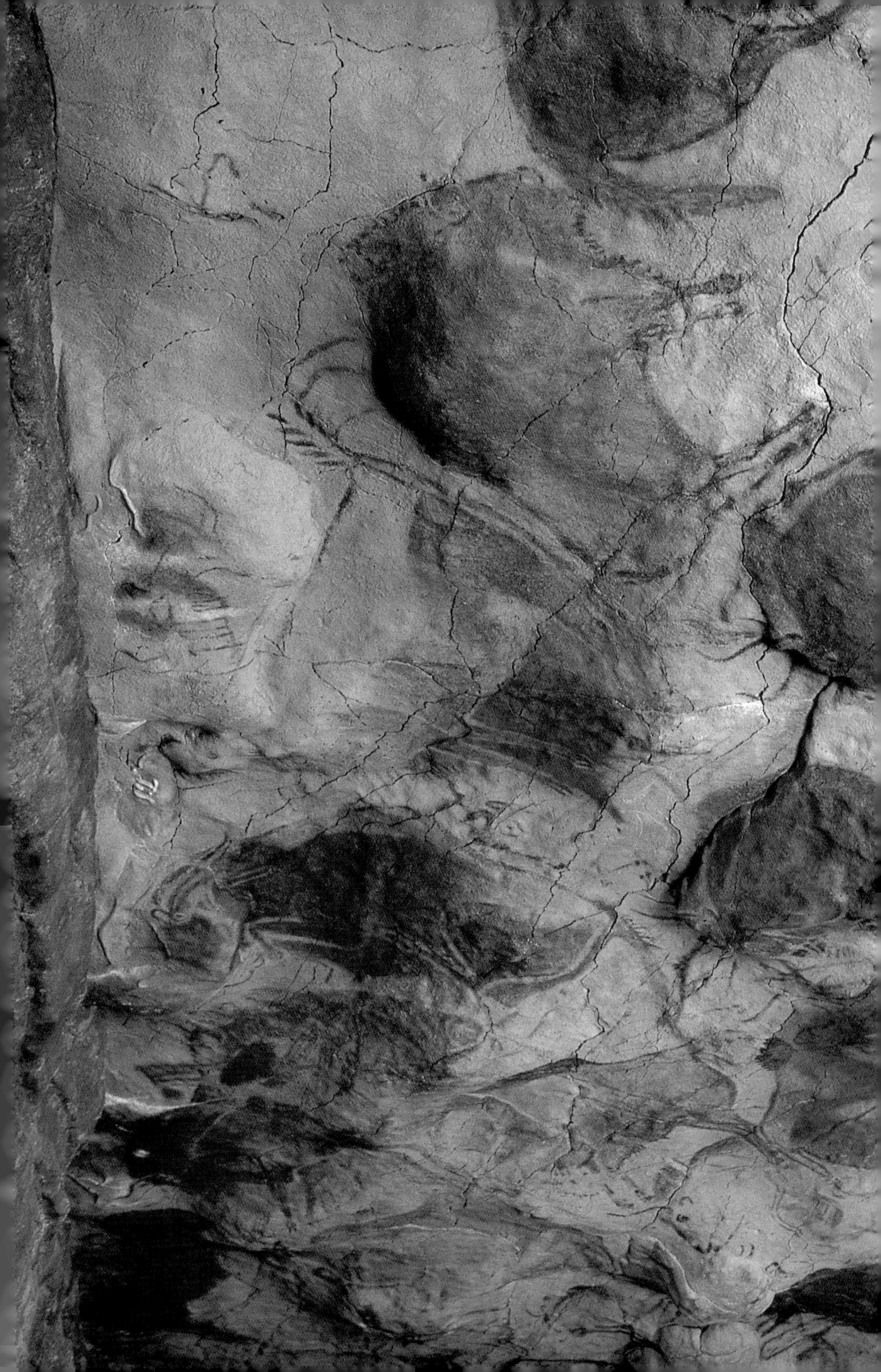

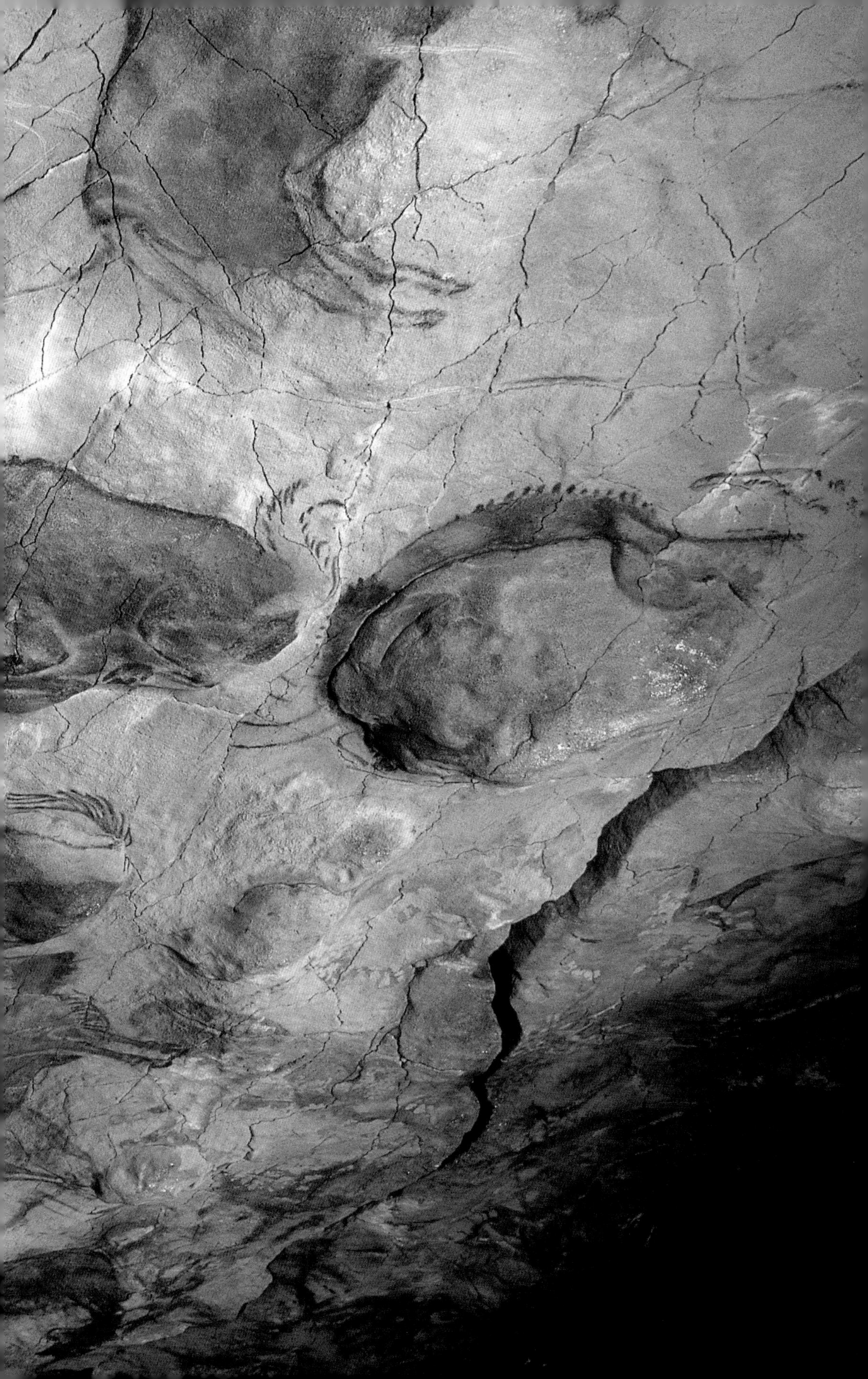

prehistorian Herminio Alcalde del Río in 1902-1904; and the very thorough digs conducted by the German Hugo Obermaier in 1924-1925. Mention should also be made of other, smaller-scale prospecting work, such as that performed in 1981 by Joaquín González Echegaray, then director of the museum, aimed basically at absolute dating; these are the most recent excavations carried out to date.

A curious feature discovered during the excavations and also reproduced at the Neocave is an ancient **bear's den** containing the fossil remains of a cave bear, perhaps an old specimen which died during hibernation and left claw marks on the floor and walls of the cave.

Further on, the **Taller del Pintor** (*Painter's Workshop*) provides an excellent introduction to the paintings we are about to see. In addition to a sample of the materials that were used – pigments of vegetable or mineral origin, and mollusk shells as recipients – visitors are shown a video that illustrates the techniques of the Paleolithic artists through the execution process of one of the famous bison of the **Polychrome Ceiling** located in the adjacent area.

This is the name which has been given to the set of paintings covering the ceiling of the room adjoining the vestibule. In the original cave, before the floor was lowered to provide access to visitors, the ceiling of this room was so low that it was impossible to stand inside it, and it therefore could never have been used as the dwelling area; this is a common feature of Paleolithic cave art, which was often located in areas that are difficult to reach, and has been interpreted as possible proof of its ritual meaning. Whatever the case, the Polychrome chamber was used for the same artistic purpose in both periods of occupation of the cave. Dating from the Solutrean is a small group of red monochrome paintings located in the part furthest away from the entrance; among others, several horses, the goat, "negative" handprints and other figures that are difficult to identify can be distinguished. The rest of the decoration of the ceiling has been ascribed to the lower Magdalenian period; it dates from approximately 14,500 years ago and mainly comprises a large herd of bison together with two horses, a large hind, perhaps a wild boar, and a series of signs known as "claviform" or club-shaped, whose meaning is uncertain. The bison are depicted in different positions: standing, lying, licking themselves, bellowing and in movement. This affords the paintings a very natural appearance and, above all, is an example of a composition in which the different figures make up a scene; this is an unusual feature in Paleolithic painting and one of the reasons why the ceiling is the jewel of Altamira and, indeed, of the whole of prehistoric art. The other is the astonishing perfection of the technique, which combines engraving, to define the outlines and certain details of the figures, and painting. Despite their name, the "Polychrome" bison of Altamira are actually done in only two pigments, black (vegetable charcoal) and red (iron oxide such as ochre or hematite), though the subsequent treatment of the figures, which were scratched or diluted in some areas to

Club-shaped signs from the Polychrome Ceiling, reproduced at the Neocave.
Pages 10-11: General view of the reproduction of the Polychrome Ceiling at the Neocave.

achieve chiaroscuro effects, gives the impression of much greater variety. If we furthermore consider the clever use of the natural contours of the support to afford the figures volume, we will appreciate the huge plastic power of the paintings, which must have been even greater when the freshness of the pigments had not yet been altered by the 14,500 years of erosion and degradation which, although undoubtedly slight, must nonetheless be taken into account.

Finally, the last section of the Neocave reproduces some of the figures from the **Horsetail**, the innermost gallery of the original cave, which is inaccessible to visitors owing to its extreme narrowness. These paintings have been dated to the lower Magdalenian period, some 14,500 years ago. They comprise horses, and deer and bison, as well as a series of abstract reticular signs known traditionally as "tectiform" on account of their supposed similarity to the roofs of huts. Here, the exploitation of the natural contours of the rock attains particular prominence, accentuated by the fact that the figures are outlined only in black, and some are astonishingly expressive, such as the frontally positioned head drawn with minimal touches of black on a projecting rock to define eyes, brows and nose.

THE MUSEUM

Sector 0: Altamira, the Discovery of Art

This area serves as an introduction to the Museum's permanent exhibition and illustrates the circumstances surrounding the discovery of the Altamira cave paintings in 1879 by Marcelino Sanz de Sautuola, a wealthy landowner with a broad interest in culture and science. Sautuola was in the habit of making excursions around the area from his house in Puente San Miguel, near Santillana, to gather insects, minerals or fossils for his collections. A reconstruction of his laboratory enables us to appreciate his wide-ranging interests, including the first cultivation of the eucalyptus tree on the Iberian Peninsula. He was also one of the pioneers in Cantabria of prehistory, then a fledgling science, and the first to excavate several caves in the region. One of them was Altamira. He learned of its existence in 1876 through one of his sharecroppers, Modesto Cubillas, who had discovered it some years previously. The vibrations from a nearby stone quarry had probably cracked the materials which had obstructed its entrance since the Paleolithic, making it practicable once again. Sautuola hastily explored the cave, managing with difficulty to reach its innermost gallery – the Horsetail – where he believed to have sighted some black drawings on the walls, though he did not pay much importance to them. However, at the Paris World's Fair in 1878 he had the chance to admire the interesting collections of prehistoric tools discovered in French caves, which encouraged him to try out his luck in those of Cantabria. The following year he began to excavate at Altamira, in the area by the cave's mouth, unearthing different stone and bone tools. According to a well-known story told by Sautuola

Figures of horses and mountain goat dating from the Solutrean, reproduced at the Neocave.

himself, while he was digging, it was actually his daughter María who spotted the paintings of the Polychrome Ceiling, exclaiming, "Daddy, oxen!" when she saw them. Sautuola wisely realised the importance of the discovery, which he expounded in a brief work published in 1880, correctly ascribing the paintings to the Paleolithic period. "Official" science was more than wary of the discovery, and there was open talk of fraud. Only a few years after Darwin's *Origin of Species* had been published, the idea that our prehistoric ancestors were capable of producing an art of such quality was regarded as contradictory to the evolutionism which the most progressive sectors of the scientific world had fervently embraced. Since Sautuola was furthermore known for his conservative ideas, it is not surprising that Emile Cartailhac, one of the most renowned figures of the time in the field of prehistory, came to regard the whole affair as a set-up intended to support creationist theories. His authority silenced the few voices raised in defence of the authenticity of Altamira until various discoveries of other similar paintings in French caves, on occasions concealed beneath unmistakably Paleolithic sediments, gradually dispelled all misgivings towards the end of the century. Cartailhac himself was forced to rectify his mistake in an article published in 1902, in which he admitted outright having contributed to "an injustice that must be recognised and publicly redressed", although this acknowledgement came too late for Sautuola, who had died in 1888.

Sector 1: Prehistoric Archaeology

The tour of the Museum's permanent exhibition begins with a brief look at the research methods of prehistoric archaeology. We are shown what the workplace of today's prehistorians is like, the process used to classify and analyse the material obtained from excavations, and the different sources from which information can be gleaned on the life of our early ancestors: remains of macrofauna and microfauna, fossil pollens, sediments, etc.

Sector 2: Before Altamira

Hominid evolution prior to the *Homo sapiens* who inhabited Altamira is the theme of this section, which tells the fascinating story of our origins over a time span of nearly two million years. It embraces the Pleistocene, the initial stage of the Quaternary period during which the genus *Homo* emerged, spread and was subsequently reduced to a single surviving species: our own.

Most of this process occurred in East Africa, where the earliest fossil hominid remains have been found. In all probability it was there where one of the many species of the genus *Australopithecus*, which spread over a considerable part of the continent during the Pliocene – between two and five million years ago – evolved into a new genus whose earliest known representatives, belonging to the species *Homo habilis*, were capable of making stone tools. Their successor, *Homo ergaster*, resembled modern man even further, not only with respect to external features such as shape of face and body

Reconstructions of Sautuola's laboratory (above) and that of a present-day archaeologist (below).

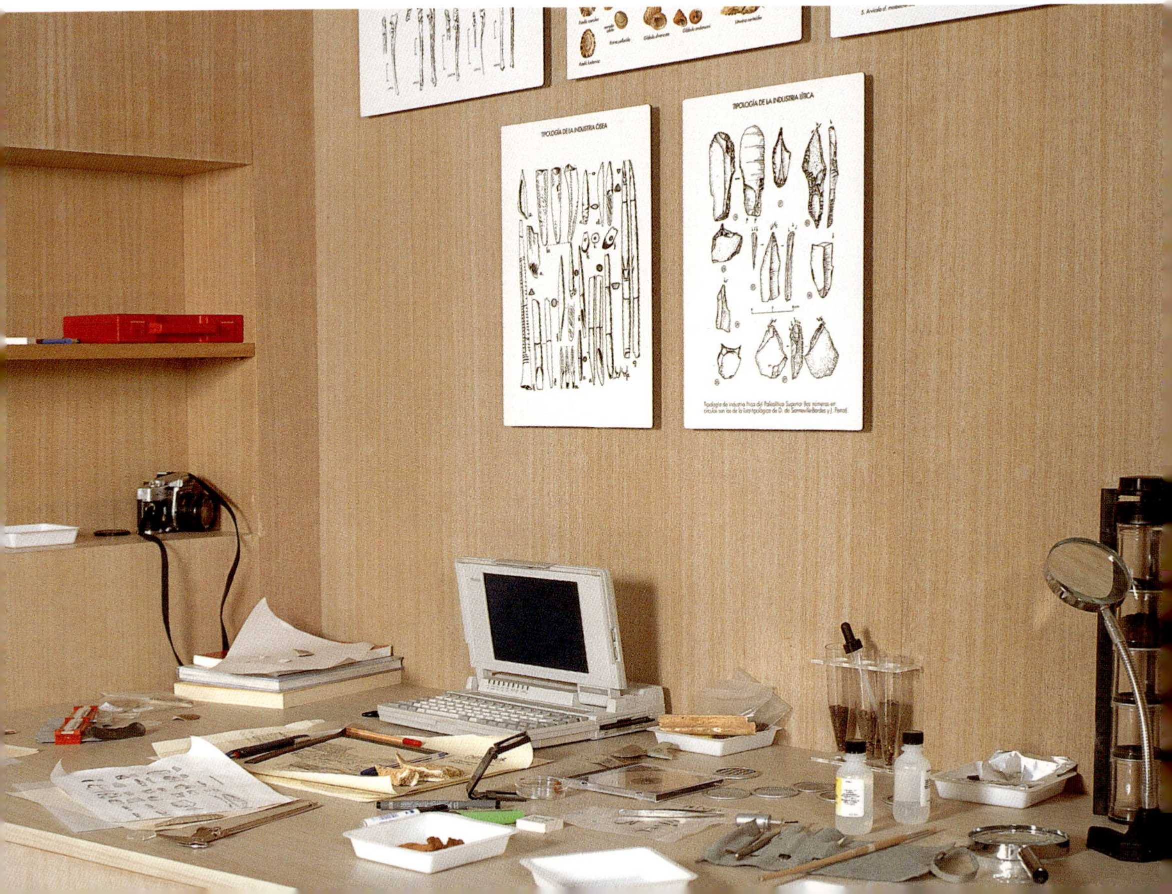
TIPOLOGÍA DE LA INDUSTRIA ÓSEA
TIPOLOGÍA DE LA INDUSTRIA LÍTICA

El primer humano,
Homo habilis
nes, elefantes,
oceerontes... ¿en Europa?
1.000.000 BP
Plioceno

lonizador
uropa,
eidelbergensis

proportions, but in other more subtle yet equally important ways relating to social and family organisation. From *H. ergaster* onwards, the evolutionary tree of the hominids branched out both taxonomically and geographically: *Homo erectus* was to populate the Asian continent and *H. antecessor* Europe – some 800,000 years ago – where he gave rise to *H. heidelbergensis*, in turn the predecessor species of *H. neanderthalensis* or the famous "Neanderthal man", a collateral branch of human evolution that coexisted with our true ancestors, the early *Homo sapiens*, for several thousands of years before becoming extinct at an unknown date, perhaps some 30,000 years ago. There is considerable evidence of the presence of Neanderthals in the caves of the Cantabrian coast that were later occupied by the *sapiens* of the Upper Paleolithic, among them Altamira, in the surroundings of which stone tools reckoned to be 100,000 years old have been found.

The hypothesis of the origin of *H. sapiens* currently regarded as the most likely is that it evolved from *H. antecessor*, though not from the European members of this species but from those who remained in Africa, and through another intermediate species, *H. rhodesiensis*. These early *sapiens* in turn spread through Asia and Europe, where they competed successfully with *H. erectus* and *H. neanderthalensis*, respectively, eventually supplanting both species.

Sector 3: Life at the Time of Altamira

The men who inhabited Altamira during the Paleolithic lived in a colder climate than today's and, consequently, were surrounded by flora and fauna similar to those currently found in the highest latitudes of Eurasia and America. The landscape alternated between herbaceous meadows and forests, particularly of conifers, though there were also birches, oaks and alder trees. As for the fauna, species still present in the region such as deer, roe deer and wild boar coexisted together with others that are no longer found – bison, horses and reindeer – or even extinct, such as the aurochs. The environment provided considerable means of subsistence, and the Paleolithic hunters were equipped to make good use of them. Their knowledge, technology and even social organisation were vastly superior to the clichéd culture generally attributed to the "cavemen". Moreover, there is evidence of a continual evolution in their way of life. The thousands of years that elapsed between the Solutrean and the Magdalenian, the two periods in which Altamira was occupied, witnessed developments in their diet – by the Magdalenian the cave dwellers were eating mollusks collected on the coast and trout or salmon caught in the rivers – and in their tools, which display a less frequent use of stone as opposed to antler and bone, which could be fashioned into more specialised implements such as harpoons and sewing needles.

As we are shown in this sector, life during the Magdalenian period basically revolved around two environments. Open spaces were territory for hunting and other activities aimed at procuring food: catching fish and shellfish and gathering plant foods

Making different antler, bone and stone implements (above) and Life at the Time of Altamira: how food was obtained (below). Pages 18-19: Sector devoted to the main hominid species that preceded Homo sapiens sapiens.

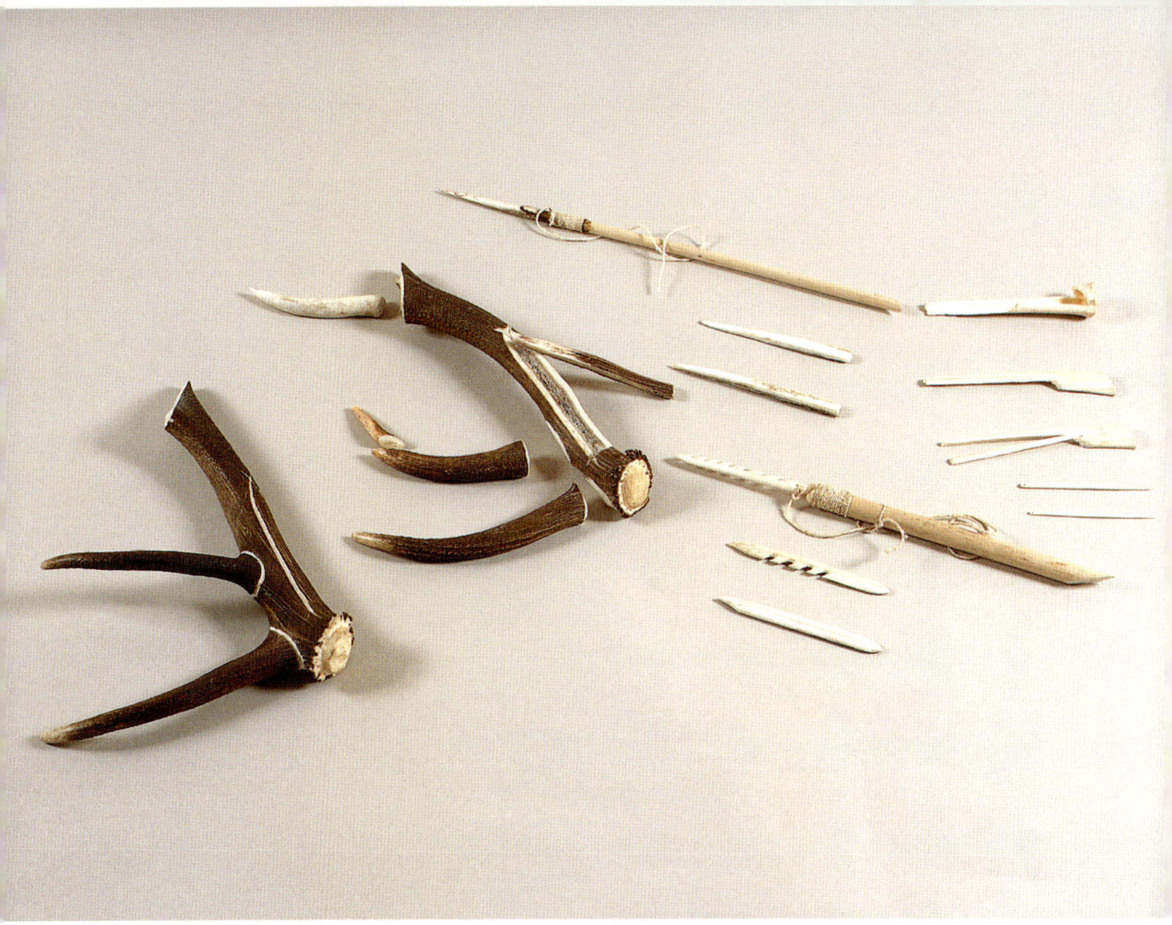

Raíces, tallos,
hojas y frutos
Pescado
y marisco
Ciervos y cabras
caballos y

such as fruit, aromatic herbs and wild mushrooms... Hunting was conducted with the use of throwing weapons: stone points during the Solutrean, and antler spearheads or points during the Magdalenian, in both cases attached to wooden handles which enabled them to be hurled by hand or using a spear-thrower. The discovery of very small stone points which could seemingly only have belonged to arrows has led to the assumption that the cave's inhabitants were also familiar with the bow, although there is no other evidence of this. The main prey were the large herbivores, especially deer, and to a lesser extent bison, goats, horses or reindeer. They occasionally hunted smaller animals such as hare or carnivores – wolves, foxes – for their skins.

Domestic chores were performed outside or inside the cave, including food processing, the tanning of hides, the sewing of garments and adornments, and tool making. The cave dwellers were familiar with the use of fire; this enabled them to roast meats, which they seasoned with aromatic herbs. Animal skins were tanned by working them at length with stone scrapers until a flexible leather was obtained that could be sewn with bone needles and thread made from gut or tendon; the garments produced were similar to those worn by Eskimos or North American Indians. In short, a life that was not lacking in certain comforts, though beset with a high mortality rate, particularly among infants, and a life expectancy of no more than thirty five: curiously enough, the same as in certain periods of the Middle Ages, despite the thousands of years which had elapsed by then. Furthermore, we should not forget that Paleolithic ways of life are not so far removed from our own environment. Even today there are peoples whose economies are based on hunting and gathering, three of which – bushmen, Eskimos and Australian aborigines – are shown in an interactive film which establishes interesting ethnographic similarities with the inhabitants of Altamira.

An important aspect of life in the Paleolithic is mobility. Ways of life based on hunting and gathering always involve some degree of nomadism, whether in pursuit of displaced prey or owing to depletion of resources in certain area. abOn occasions, these are only brief displacements made by the hunters chasing their prey, and on others the whole human group move, taking with them all their material belongings, to settle in another place for a period of time of varying length.

The major sanctuaries of Cantabrian Paleolithic art constitute interesting examples of the different types of occupation relating to this form of life. Thus, the cave of Rascaño, located in a mountainous area, appears to have been used as a seasonal shelter during the spring and summer months when the mountain goat was hunted, the species to which most of the bone remains found in it belong. By contrast, El Juyo would have been a permanent settlement in an area ideally suited to a combination of deer hunting and catching fish and shellfish, like El Castillo, one of the most interesting caves in Cantabria, where the longer time span of the materials found seems to indicate that it was used as a base camp from the first

Remains of deer, mollusks and bone, antler and stone tools from El Juyo (above) and life at the Time of Altamira: activities performed in the dwelling area (below).

Artesanía
de la piel
Lo último
en moda

settlement in the region to the last one of the glacial era by both Neanderthal man and by *Homo sapiens*. As for Altamira, the theory has been put forward that it was a "gathering place" where normally dispersed human groups met with a certain periodicity, perhaps to perform some kind of ritual.

The final part of this sector deals with death in the Paleolithic world – a theme about which little is still known, as the burial sites found are very scarce, though sufficient to indicate that there was some type of belief in life after death. Images of some Paleolithic burials, both individual and collective, found in different parts of Europe show how the corpses were prepared, accompanied by their possessions and food, and occasionally covered in an ochre layer.

Sector 4: The Earliest Art

Analysing artistic manifestations is a key part of any approach to the Paleolithic world, though particularly in the case of Altamira owing to the excellence of its paintings. One of the first problems encountered when studying these is dating the works, which are simply found on the walls and the ceilings of the caves and provide no additional information – such as, in the case of movable art obtained through excavations, the geological strata in which they are located – that could help ascertain when they were executed. Nowadays we possess highly reliable dating methods, such as carbon 14, which allows the age of organic remains to be calculated up to a maximum of 40,000 years and can be employed in paintings where vegetable charcoal is used and also, indirectly, to date engravings done on bone which can be ascribed chronologically to paintings executed using the same technique. Such is the case of Altamira, where the excavations have unearthed several deer shoulder blades on which drawings, mainly of deer's heads, are engraved, using a technique of striping and streaking to shape and give volume to the inner part of the figures. The same technique is found in images of deer engraved on the walls of the Horsetail, as well as in other caves in the central area of the Cantabrian coast, where this technique is widespread, and constitutes an interesting variation within the general homogeneity of Cantabrian Paleolithic art.

Engraving was widely used in art throughout the whole period, either on its own or together with painting, to define the outline of the figures onto which the pigments were subsequently applied. These pigments were mainly mineral in origin, the only exception being the vegetable charcoal used for the black strokes. The most common were iron oxide – ochre, hematite – which, combined with other elements, could produce an extremely broad range of yellows, reds and browns. They were applied with fingers, or using fur pads or rags, and in some more elaborate cases (the Polychrome Ceiling at Altamira) tonal variations were introduced by scraping or partial rinsing. A special technique was used to produce the "negative" imprints of hands that are found in many caves, a sort of airbrush effect achieved by blowing paint onto the wall through small tubes made from birds' bones.

Drawings of a bison (above) and the head of a large bovid (below) executed in black pigment, reproduction at the Neocave.

The handprints, both "negative" and "positive", are among the most enigmatic images of this art, the significance of which basically escapes us. Animals, signs and human figures, listed in order of abundance, are the three main themes in Paleolithic cave art. The most frequently represented animals are deer, horses, bison, aurochs, reindeer and goats... that is, the herbivores which constituted Paleolithic hunters' usual prey, and this initially gave rise to the theory that the paintings served a ritual purpose, perhaps to encourage successful hunting. However, there is not always a direct relationship between the most commonly represented animals and those most frequently hunted by the inhabitants according to the records of the bones found in excavations. In Altamira, for example, most of the remains found belong to deer, whereas bison are the most commonly depicted animal.

More mysterious still are the signs, which have been given names – tectiform, claviform, scalariform (ladderlike) – that indicate the prehistorians' perplexity vis-à-vis these figures, any interpretation of which must necessarily remain within the realm of hypothesis. One of the most recent ones considers the club-shaped signs of the Polychrome Ceiling at Altamira to be symbols of female fertility.

The human forms, generally few and far between in Paleolithic art, are always very schematic and contrast greatly with the naturalism of the animal representations. They are often limited to parts of the body, such as vulvas and, in particular, hands, imprints of which are found in abundance in two forms: positive – a paint-smeared hand is pressed on the rock – and negative, in which the silhouette of the hand is produced by means of an airbrush technique.

In this sector we are shown a glimpse of other major sanctuaries of Paleolithic art in Cantabria through the facsimiles of four caves which display the variety of themes and techniques developed in the different ages of the Upper Paleolithic. From the Fuente del Salín cave is a reproduction of a panel of negative handprints dated between 25,000 and 20,000 years ago. El Pendo displays the technique of stamping with a red pigment used in the Solutrean through the figures of hinds, a goat, a horse and different signs which are between 22,000 and 18,000 years old. Cueva de las Monedas illustrates the end of cave art (12,000 years ago) through a horse and reindeer drawn in charcoal; the presence of the reindeer indicates that these belong to the last glacial period prior to the climatic change which marked the transition to the Holocene. A reproduction from the cave of Chufín in Rionansa, Cantabria, shows a panel of goats and deer which were carved out of the limestone using flint gravers between 25,000 and 18,000 years ago.

We next come to the Museum's important collection of portable art, enriched with items on loan from other museums. The exhibits are arranged into five sections. The first comprises implements and tools: points, harpoons, spearheads and gravers... The second includes implements that obviously served the purpose of adornment, that is, carved items with a hole in them which identifies them as pendants. The third and fifth

Reproduction of a fragment of the cave at Fuente del Salín showing "negative" handprints. Pages 26-27: Bison from the Polychrome Ceiling adapted to the natural contours of the rock, reproduction at the Neocave.

sections deal with two types of implements whose use is unknown, though their abundance leads us to assume they played a prominent role in the Paleolithic world: the perforated bars or pieces of bone of a certain size that are decorated and have holes drilled in one of their ends, and the deer shoulder blades engraved with animal drawings. Finally, there is a section – the fourth – displaying a variety of decorated objects whose use is also unknown.

The last part of this sector, devoted to music, mainly features the flutes found in the French Basque cave of Isturitz, together with examples of other Paleolithic musical instruments such as bull-roarers, and the sounds produced by them all.

Sector 5: The End of an Era

As mentioned earlier on, an overall warming of the planet took place some 10,000 years ago, altering Paleolithic man's environment considerably. As a result of the melting of the glacial ice the sea level rose, causing the coastline to retreat some 5-6 kilometres landward in the area in question. Conifer forests were replaced by deciduous ones, the large herbivores associated with cold climates, such as bison and reindeer, migrated northwards, and species still found in the area today – deer, roe deer and wild boar – became predominant.

This transition period between the Pleistocene and the Holocene is known in prehistoric archaeology as the Azilian and has been dated between 11,000 and 9,000 years ago. It is characterised by a much more sober industry: undecorated harpoons, a drastic reduction in the size of the stone implements and the disappearance of the great Paleolithic art, which was replaced by much cruder manifestations such as smooth edges decorated with non-figurative representations. There is evidence of a greater exploitation of coastal resources, with the incorporation of new species such as mussels, crabs and sea urchins into the diet, and of lesser mobility of the populations, which translated into a regional diversification of cultural manifestations, breaking the unity that Paleolithic nomadism fostered. This was the first step towards sedentarisation, which was to become further consolidated as agriculture and animal husbandry developed during the Neolithic period.

Sector 6: More Prehistory

A notice board with press clippings on prehistory in general and Altamira in particular, supplementary information about other sites in the area, and a brief examination of the influence of the Prehistoric world on different fields of our own age, such as the film industry, comics, advertising and art, comprise this sector which brings the Altamira Museum's permanent exhibition to a close.

Examples of portable art from the Magdalenian: perforated antler bars (above) and Azilian antler harpoons (below).

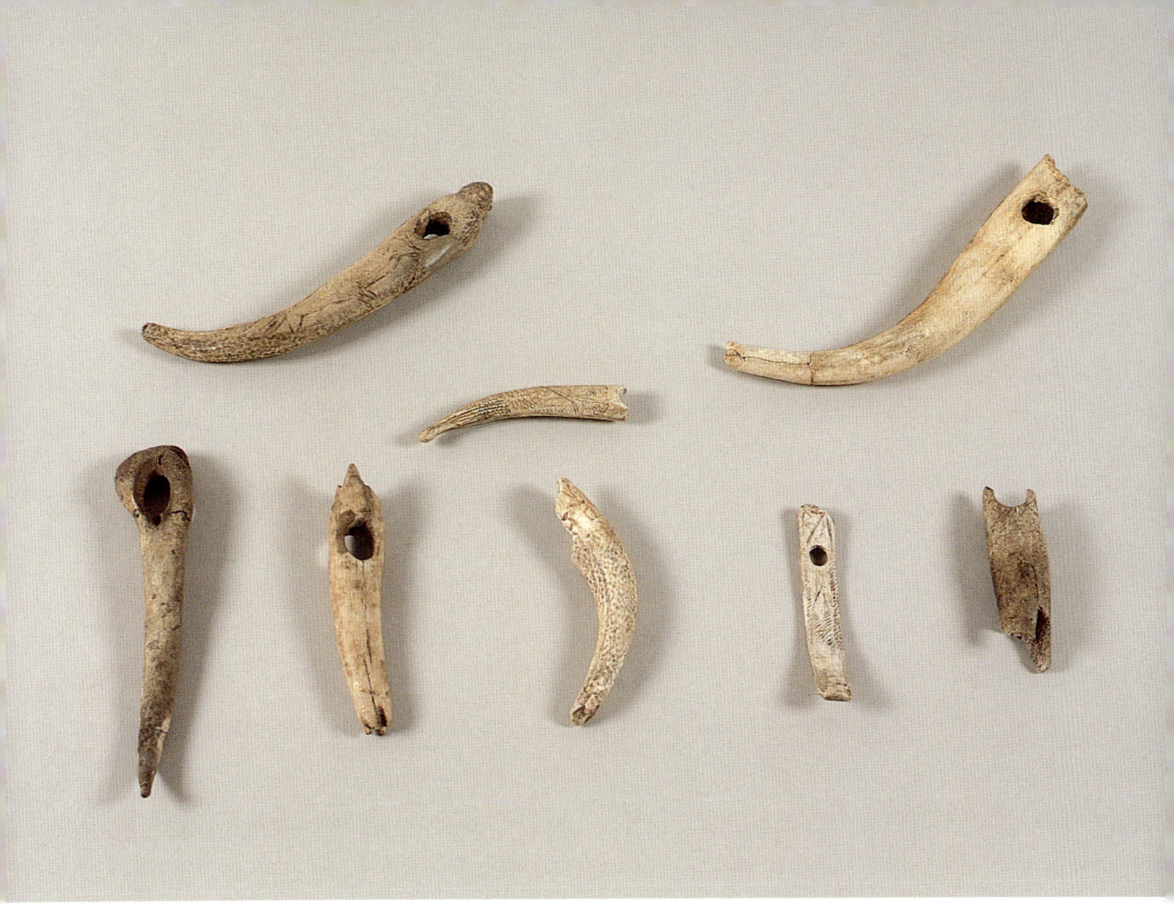

I.S.B.N.: 84-8003-931-0
D.L.: M-33569-2004
Photographs: © Pedro Saura
(pages: Portada, 5, 7, 10-11, 13, 15, 25)
© Bustamante Hurtado (pages: 9, 17, 18-19,
21, 23, 26-27, 29, 31 and back cover)

Published and produced by: Aldeasa
Text: Ana Martín Moreno
Translation: Jenny Dodman
Colecction design: A. Ochoa de Zabalegui
Layout: Aldeasa
Photomecanical production: Lucam
Printesd by: Jomagar

Cover: *Motionless bison, reproduction of the main Panel, Polychrome Chamber.*
Back cover: *View of the exterior of the Museum. Architect: Juan Navarro Baldeweg.*